Strum It GUITAR

AUTHENTIC CHORDS
ORIGINAL KEYS
COMPLETE SONGS

Taylor Swift
FOR ACOUSTIC GUITAR

Cover photo by Sarah Barlow © Big Machine Records

ISBN 978-1-4768-7127-1

HAL•LEONARD® CORPORATION

7777 W. BLUEMOUND RD. P.O. BOX 13819 MILWAUKEE, WI 53213

Visit Hal Leonard Online at
www.halleonard.com

Back to December

Words and Music by Taylor Swift

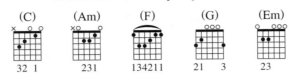

Capo II

Intro

Moderately slow

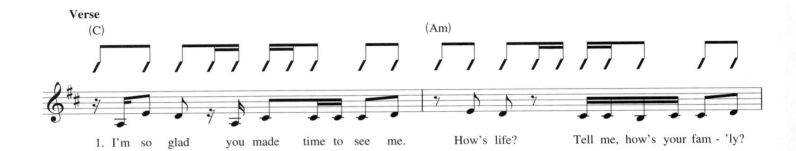

*Symbols in parentheses represent chord names respective to capoed guitar and do not reflect actual sounding chords.

Verse

1. I'm so glad you made time to see me. How's life? Tell me, how's your fam-'ly?

I have-n't seen them in a while. You've been good, bus-i-er than ev-er

**Symbols in parentheses represent chord names respective to capoed guitar.
Symbols above reflect actual sounding chords..

with small talk, work and the weath-er. Your guard is up and I know why.

Pre-Chorus

Be-cause the last time you saw me is still burned in the back of your mind. You gave me

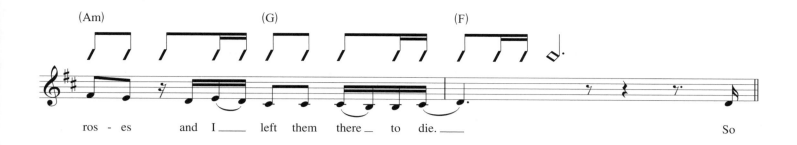

ros - es and I ____ left them there ___ to die. ____ So

𝄋 Chorus

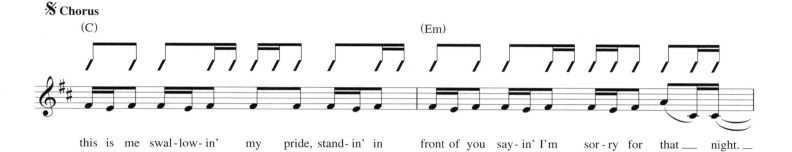

this is me swal-low-in' my pride, stand-in' in front of you say-in' I'm sor-ry for that ___ night. ___

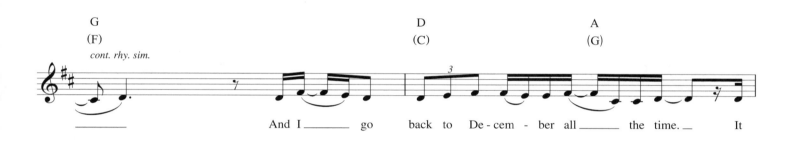

____ And I ____ go back to De - cem - ber all ____ the time. ___ It

turns out free-dom ain't noth-in' but miss-in' you, wish-in' I'd re-al-ized what I had ___ when you ___

To Coda ⊕

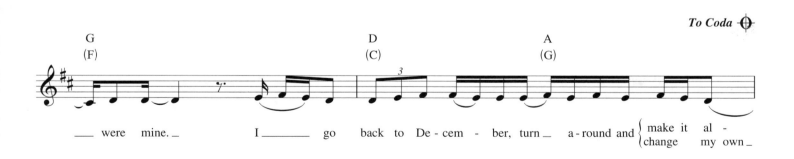

___ were mine. _ I ____ go back to De - cem - ber, turn ___ a-round and {make it al - / change my own ___

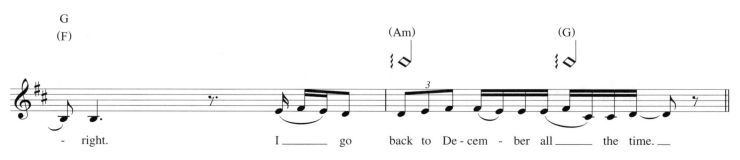

- right. I ____ go back to De - cem - ber all ____ the time. ___

Interlude

Verse

2. These days   I have-n't been sleep-in'.   Stay-in' up play-in' back _ my - self leav - in'.

G
(F)

cont. rhy. sim.

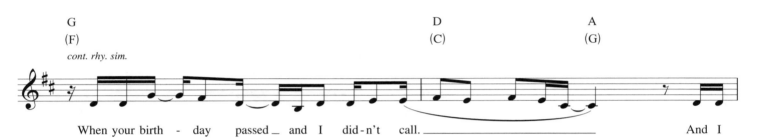

When your birth - day   passed _ and I   did-n't   call. _____   And I

D
(C)

think a - bout sum-mer, all the beau-ti - ful   times _   I   watched you laugh-in' from the pas - sen-ger   side   and

G
(F)

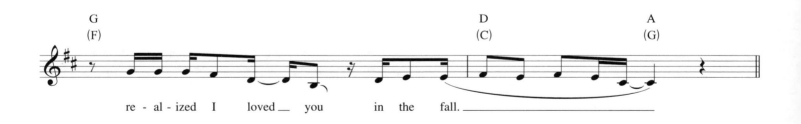

re - al - ized I   loved _ you   in   the   fall. _____

Pre-Chorus

Bm   A   D   G
(Am)   (G)   (C)   (F)

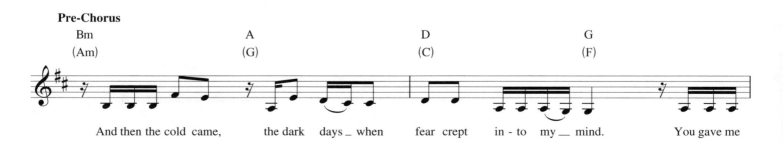

And then the cold came,   the dark   days _ when   fear crept   in - to   my _ mind.   You gave me

4

all your love ___ and all I gave you was good - bye. ___ So

Coda

___ mind. I ___ go back to De - cem - ber all ___ the time. ___

Interlude

Bridge

I miss ___ your tan skin, ___ your sweet smile. ___ So

good to me, ___ so ___ right. And how you held ___ me in ___ your arms ___ that Sep - tem - ber night, ___

___ the first time ___ you ___ ev - er saw ___ me ___ cry. ___ May - be this is wish - ful think - in',

prob - a - bly mind - less dream - in'. But, if we loved a - gain __ I swear I'd love __ you

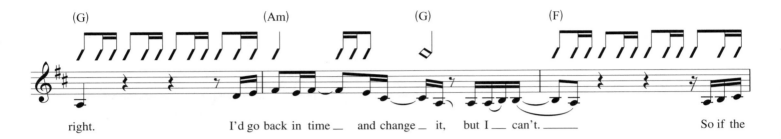

right. I'd go back in time __ and change __ it, but I __ can't. __ So if the

chain is on __ your door, __ I un - der - stand. __ But

Chorus

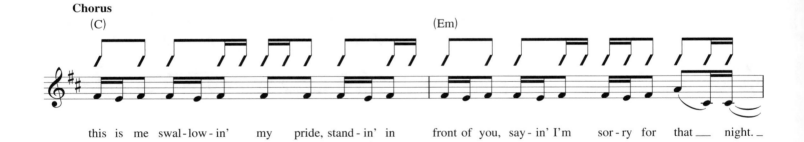

this is me swal - low - in' my pride, stand - in' in front of you, say - in' I'm sor - ry for that __ night. __

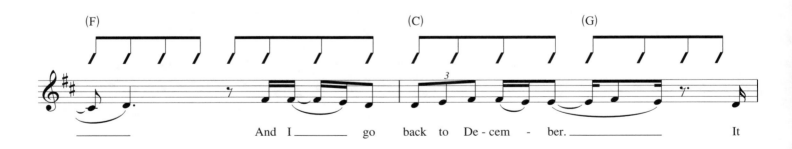

__ And I __ go back to De - cem - ber. __ It

turns out free - dom ain't noth - in' but miss - in' you, wish - in' I'd re - al - ized what I had __ when you __

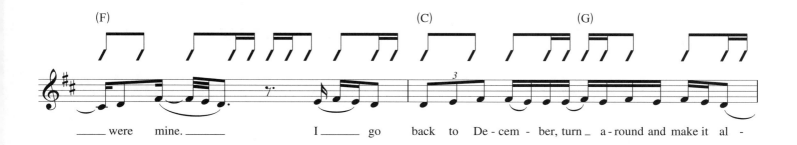

_____ were mine. _____ I _____ go back to De - cem - ber, turn _ a - round and make it al -

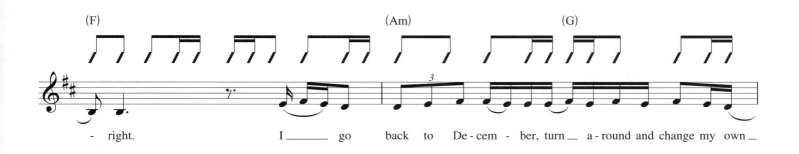

- right. I _____ go back to De - cem - ber, turn _ a - round and change my own _____

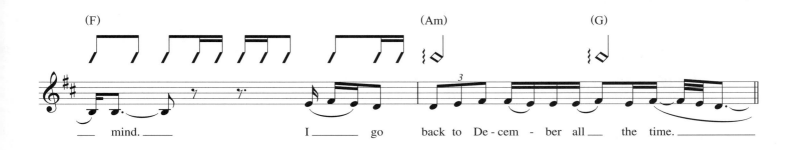

_____ mind. _____ I _____ go back to De - cem - ber all _____ the time. _____

Outro

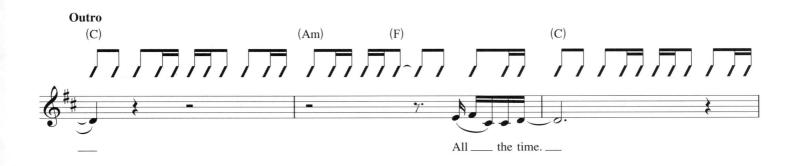

_____ All _____ the time. _____

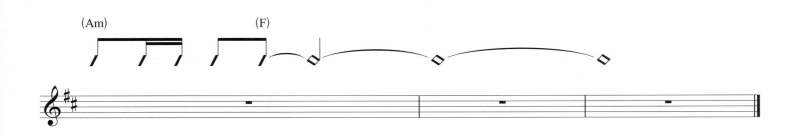

Better Than Revenge

Words and Music by Taylor Swift

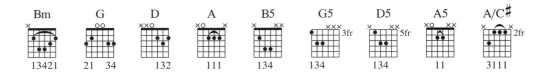

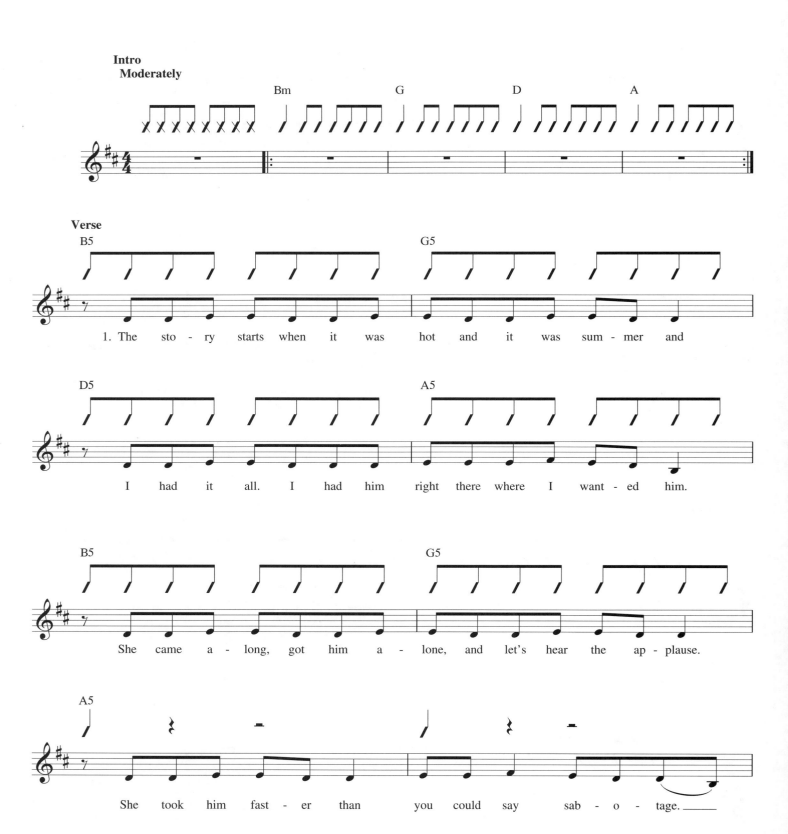

I nev-er saw it com-ing, nor did I sus-pect it. I un-der-es-ti-mat-ed

just who I was deal-ing with. She had to know the pain was beat-ing on me like a drum.

She un-der-es-ti-mat-ed just who she was steal-ing from.

𝄋 Chorus

She's not a saint and she's not what you think, she's an ac-tress, whoa. But

she's bet-ter known for the things that she does on the mat-tress, whoa.

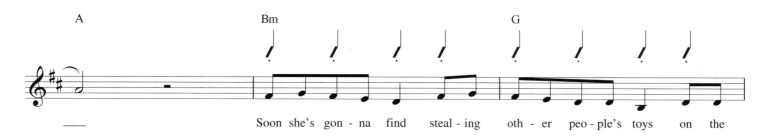

Soon she's gon-na find steal-ing oth-er peo-ple's toys on the

play - ground won't make you man - y friends. _ She should keep in mind, she should

To Coda ⊕

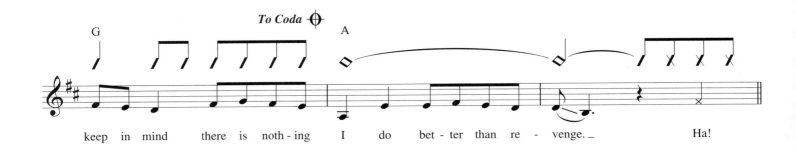

keep in mind there is noth - ing I do bet - ter than re - venge. _ Ha!

Interlude

Verse

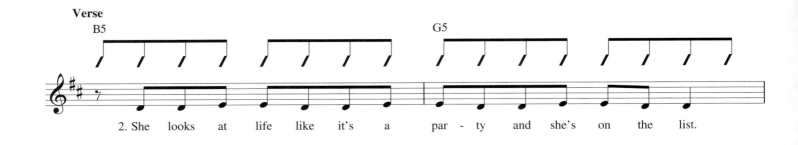

2. She looks at life like it's a par - ty and she's on the list.

cont. rhy. sim.

She looks at me like I'm a trend and she's so o - ver it.

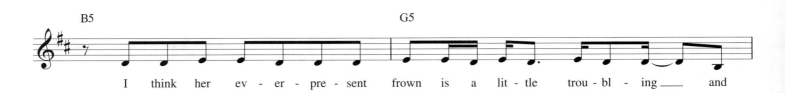

I think her ev - er - pre - sent frown is a lit - tle trou - bl - ing ____ and

she think's I'm psy-cho 'cause I like to rhyme her name with things.

But so-phis-ti-ca-tion is-n't what you wear or who you know

or push-ing peo-ple down to get you where you wan-na go. ___

They did-n't teach you that in prep school, so it's up to me. But no a-mount of vin-tage

D.S. al Coda

dress-es gives you dig-ni-ty. ___ Yeah,

Coda

I do bet-ter than re-venge. ___ I'm

Bridge

just an-oth-er thing for you to roll your eyes ___ at, hon-ey. You might have him, ___ but

have-n't you ___ heard? I'm just an-oth-er thing for you to roll your eyes ___ at, hon-ey. You

might have ___ him, but I al-ways get the last ___ word, ___

___ oo, word, ___ whoa. ___

She's not a saint and she's not what you think. She's an

ac - tress, whoa. ___

She's bet-ter known for the things that she does on the mat-tress, whoa. ___

*Previous 2 meas.

12

Eyes Open

from THE HUNGER GAMES
Words and Music by Taylor Swift

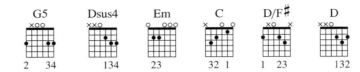

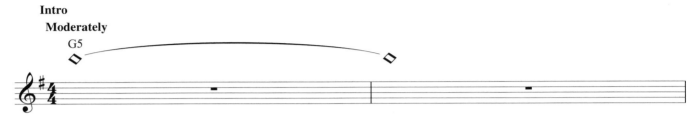

Intro
Moderately

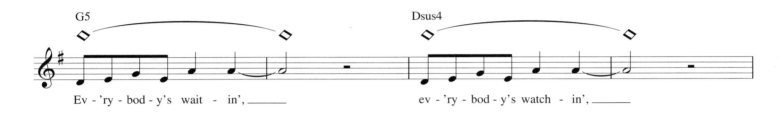

Ev - 'ry - bod - y's wait - in', _____ ev - 'ry - bod - y's watch - in', _____

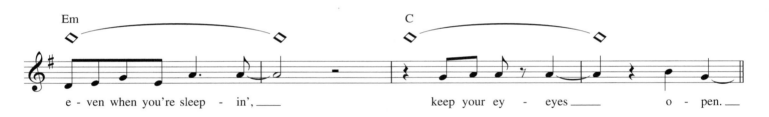

e - ven when you're sleep - in', _____ keep your ey - eyes _____ o - pen. _____

Interlude
Half-time feel

cont. rhy. sim.

Verse

1. The trick - y thing is yes - ter - day we were just chil - dren play - ing sol - diers just pre -

tend - ing, dream - ing dreams with hap - py _____ end - ings. _____

In back yards, win - ning bat - tles with our wood - en swords,

but now we've stepped in - to a cruel _ world, where ev - 'ry - bod - y stands

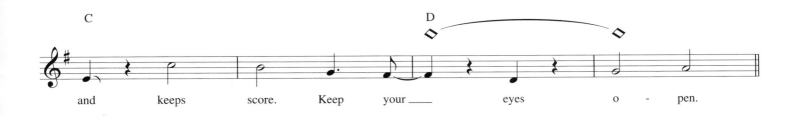

and keeps score. Keep your _____ eyes o - pen.

Chorus

Ev - 'ry - bod - y's wait - in' _____ for you to break down, ev - 'ry - bod - y's watch - in' _____

_____ to see the fall - out, e - ven when you're sleep - in', sleep - i - in',

keep your ey - eyes _____ o - pen. _____

Keep your ey - eyes _____ o - pen, _____

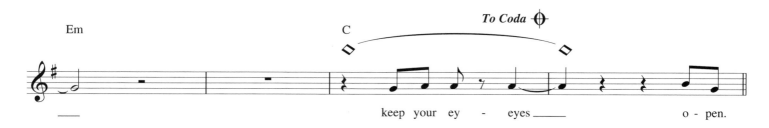

To Coda ⊕

_____ keep your ey - eyes _____ o - pen.

Interlude

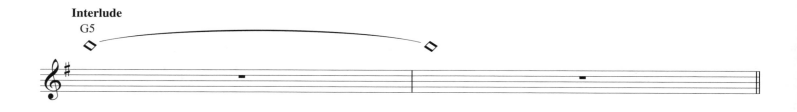

Verse

cont. rhy. sim.

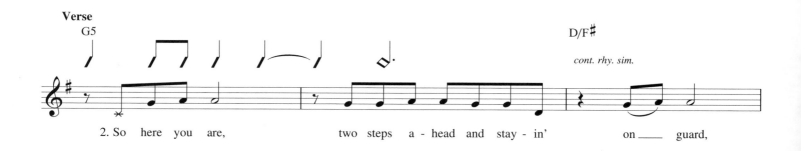

2. So here you are, two steps a - head and stay - in' on ___ guard,

ev - 'ry les - son forms a new scar they nev - er thought you'd make it,

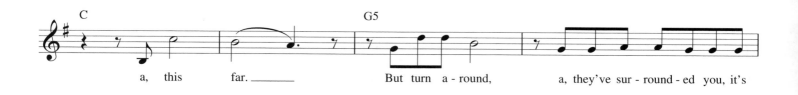

a, this far. _____ But turn a - round, a, they've sur - round - ed you, it's

a show down and no - bod - y comes to save you now, but you've got some - thing they don't,

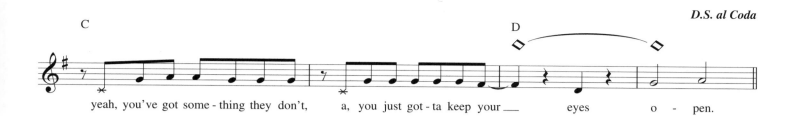

yeah, you've got some-thing they don't,   a, you just got-ta keep your ___ eyes   o - pen.

Coda

Bridge

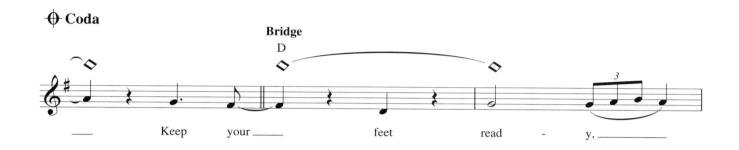

___ Keep   your ___   feet   read - y, _____

heart - beat   stead - y, _____   keep   your

eyes _____   o - pen.   Keep ___

your   aim   locked,   the ___ night   goes   dark,   keep _____

___ your   eyes _____   o - pen. ___

Interlude

Outro-Chorus

Ev - 'ry - bod - y's wait - in' _____ for you to break down. Ev - 'ry - bod - y's watch - in' _____

_____ to see the fall - out, e - ven when you're sleep - in', sleep - i - in',

keep your ey - eyes _____ o - pen. Keep your ey -

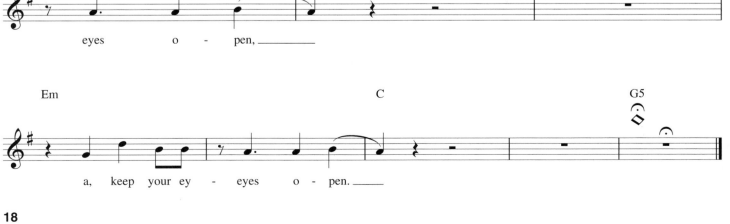

eyes o - pen, _____

a, keep your ey - eyes o - pen. _____

Love Story

Words and Music by Taylor Swift

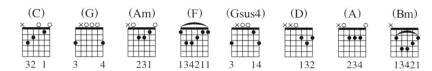

Capo II

Intro
Moderately

*Symbols in parentheses represent chord names respective to capoed guitar and do not reflect actual sounding chords.

Verse

1. We were both young when I first saw ___ you. I close my eyes ___ and the

**Symbols in parentheses represent chord names respective to capoed guitar.
Symbols above reflect actual sounding chords.

flash - back starts. ___ I'm stand - ing there on a bal - co - ny in

sum - mer air. See the lights, ___ see the par - ty, the ball ___ gowns. See you make ___ your way through the crowd ___ and say hel -

lo. Lit-tle did I _____ know that

Pre-Chorus
you were Ro-me-o. You were throw-ing peb - bles and my dad-dy said, "Stay a-way from

Ju - li - et." And I was cry-ing on the stair - case, beg-ging you, "Please, _ don't go." _

Chorus
_____ And I _____ said, "Ro - me - o, take _ me

some-where we can be a - lone. I'll be wait - ing; all there's left to do is run.

You'll be the prince and I'll be the prin - cess. It's a love sto - ry. _ Ba - by, just say yes." _

Interlude
_ 2. So

20

Fifteen

Words and Music by Taylor Swift

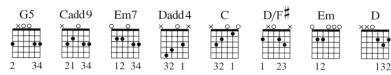

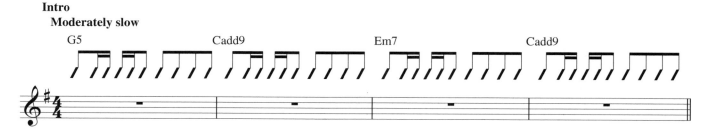

Intro
Moderately slow

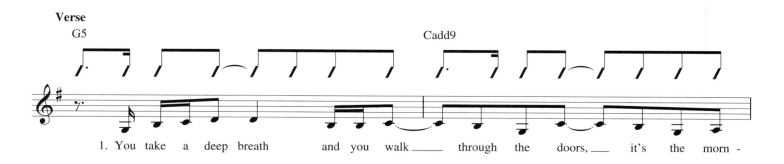

1. You take a deep breath and you walk ___ through the doors, ___ it's the morn-

ing of your ver-y first day. ___ You say hi to your friends ___ you ain't

seen in a while, ___ try and stay out of ev-'ry-bod-y's way.

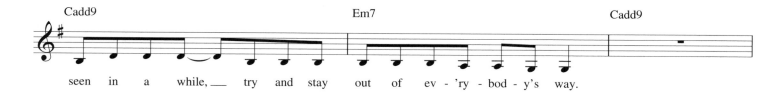

It's your fresh-man year and you're gon-na be ___ here ___ for the next ___ four years in this

town. Hop-ing one of those ___ sen-ior boys ___ will wink at you and say, ___ "You know, I

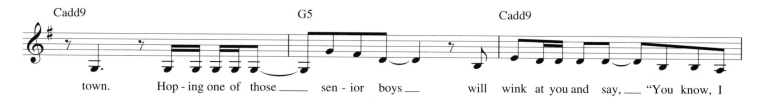

think-ing he's ___ the one, ___ and you're danc - ing 'round the room ___ when the night

D.S. al Coda 1

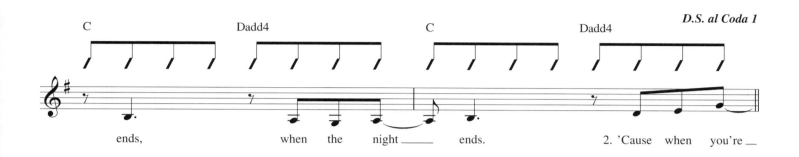

ends, when the night ___ ends. 2. 'Cause when you're ___

Coda 1

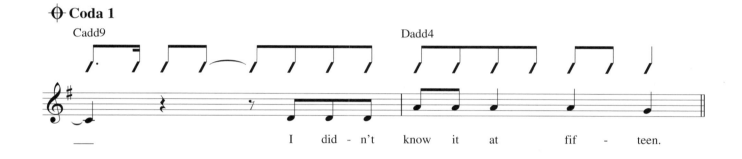

___ I did - n't know it at fif - teen.

Guitar Solo

Bridge

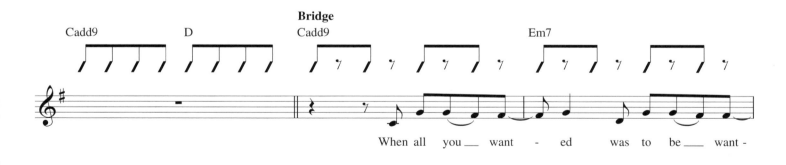

When all you ___ want - ed was to be ___ want -

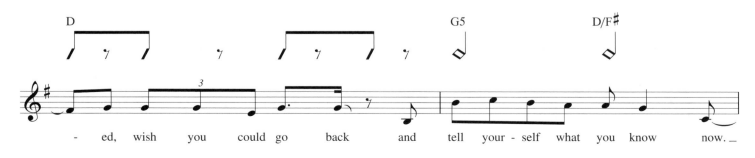

- ed, wish you could go back and tell your-self what you know now. ___

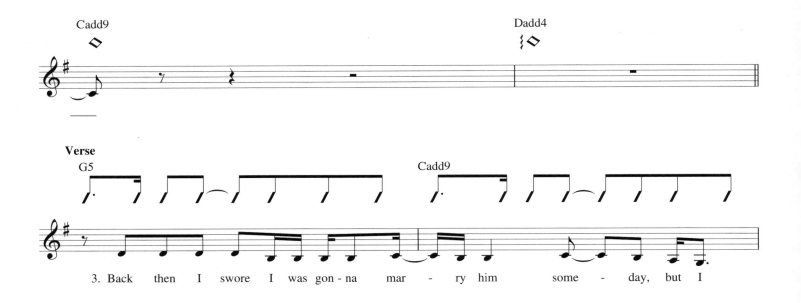

Verse

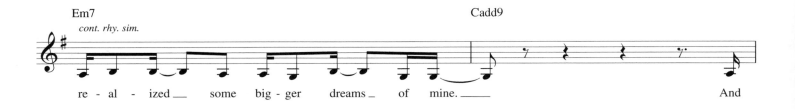

3. Back then I swore I was gon-na mar - ry him some - day, but I

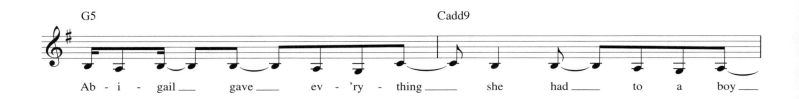

re - al - ized __ some big - ger dreams __ of mine. _____ And

Ab - i - gail __ gave __ ev - 'ry - thing __ she had __ to a boy __

D.S. al Coda 2

__ who changed his __ mind, __ and we both cried. __ 3. 'Cause when you're_

⊕ Coda 2

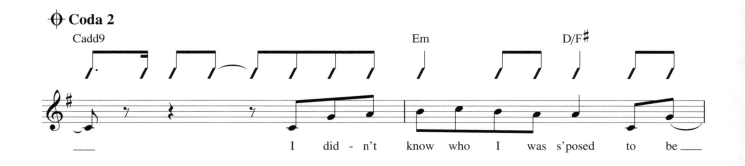

__ I did - n't know who I was s'posed to be __

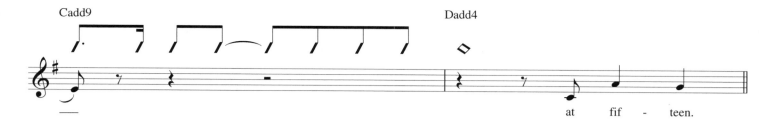

Cadd9   Dadd4

at fif - teen.

Outro

G5   Cadd9   Em7

La, la, la, ___ la, la, la, ___

C   G5   Cadd9   Em7

___ la,   la, ___ la, ___ la.   La, la, la, ___ la, la, la, ___ la,   la, ___ la, ___ la.   La, la, la, ___ la, la, la. ___

Cadd9   G5   Cadd9

___ Your ver - y first ___ day.   Uh, take a deep breath, girl. ___

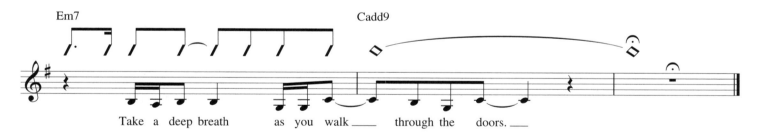

Em7   Cadd9

Take a deep breath   as you walk ___ through the doors. ___

Additional Lyrics

Chorus 2. 'Cause when you're fifteen
       And somebody tells you they love you,
       You're gonna believe them.
       And when you're fifteen,
       And your first kiss makes your head spin 'round.
       But in your life you'll do things greater than
       Dating the boy on the football team.
       I didn't know it at fifteen.

Chorus 3. 'Cause when you're fifteen
       And somebody tells you they love you,
       You're gonna believe them.
       And when you're fifteen,
       Don't forget to look before you fall.
       I've found time can heal most anything,
       And you just might find who you're supposed to be.
       I didn't know who I was s'posed to be at fifteen.

Mean

Words and Music by Taylor Swift

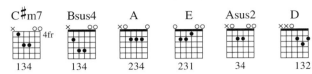

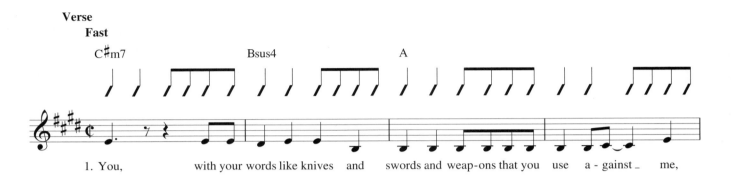

Verse
Fast

1. You, with your words like knives and swords and weap-ons that you use a-gainst __ me,

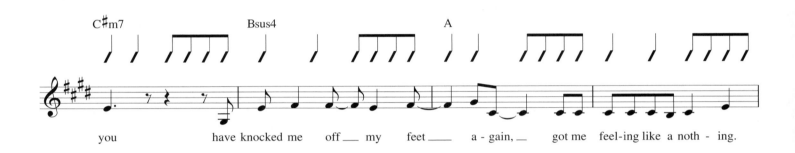

you have knocked me off __ my feet __ a-gain, __ got me feel-ing like a noth - ing.

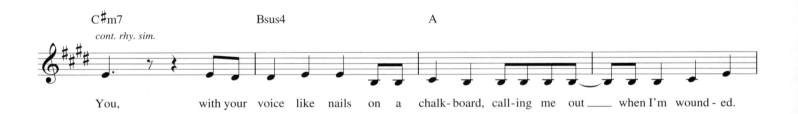

You, with your voice like nails on a chalk-board, call-ing me out __ when I'm wound - ed.

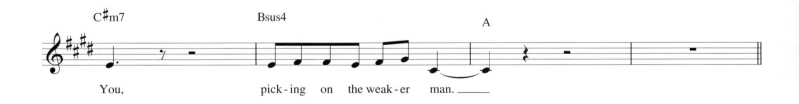

You, pick-ing on the weak - er man. _____

Pre-Chorus

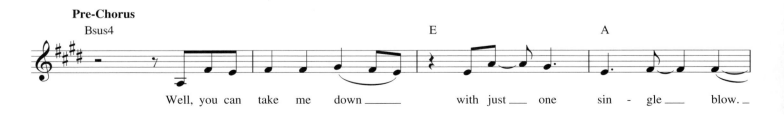

Well, you can take me down _____ with just __ one sin - gle __ blow. _

But you ___ don't know, ___ what you ___ don't know. ___

Chorus

Some - day, ___ I'll be liv - in' in a big ol' cit - y and

all you're ___ ev - er gon - na be is mean.

Some - day, ___ I'll be big e - nough so you can't hit me and

To Coda

all you're ___ ev - er gon - na be is mean. Why you got - ta be so ___

Interlude

___ mean?

Verse

2. You, with your switch - ing sides and your wild - fire lies and your hu - mil - i - a - tion,

C#m7　　　　　Bsus4　　　　　　　　A

you,　　have point-ed out __ my flaws __ a-gain, __ as if I don't al-read-y see them.

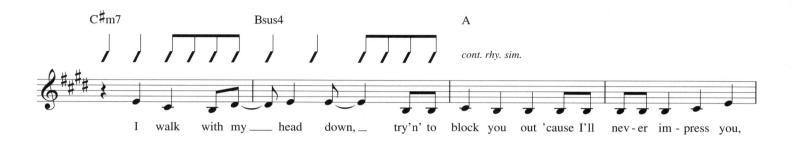

C#m7　　　　　　　Bsus4　　　　　　　　A

cont. rhy. sim.

I walk with my __ head down, __ try'n' to block you out 'cause I'll nev-er im-press you,

C#m7　　　　　Bsus4　　　　　　　A

I　　just wan-na feel o-kay __ a-gain. __

Pre-Chorus

Bsus4　　　　　　　　　　　　　E　　　　　A

I bet you got pushed a - round, _____ some-bod-y made you __ cold.

Bsus4　　　　　　　　　　　　　　A

But the cy-cle ends __ right now, _____ 'cause you can't lead __ me down __

D.S. al Coda

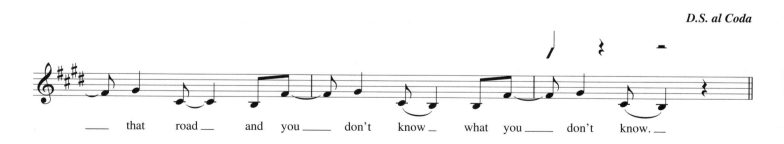

__ that road __ and you __ don't know __ what you __ don't know. __

⊕ Coda

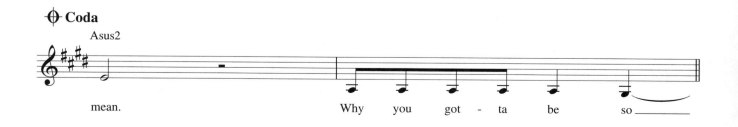

Asus2

mean.　　　　　　　Why you got-ta be so ____

Interlude

____ mean.   All   you   are ___ is

mean   and   a   li - ar   and pa - thet - ic   and a - lone in life ___ and

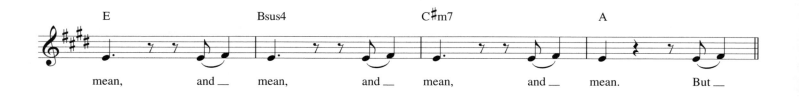

mean,   and __ mean,   and __ mean,   and __ mean.   But __

Chorus

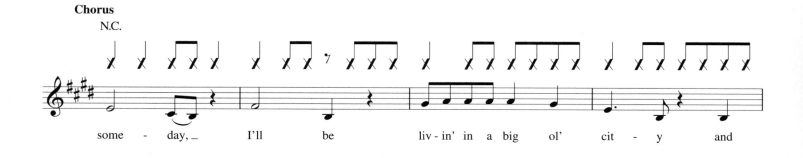

some - day, __   I'll   be   liv - in' in a big ol' cit - y   and

all   you're __   ev - er gon - na be   is   mean.   Yeah! _____

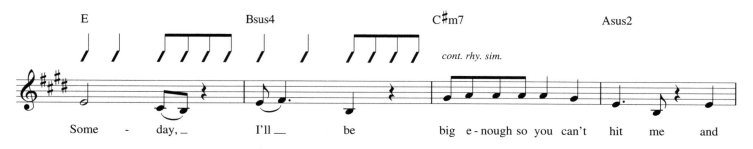

Some - day, __   I'll __   be   big e - nough so you can't hit me   and

all you're ___ ev - er gon - na be is mean.

Chorus

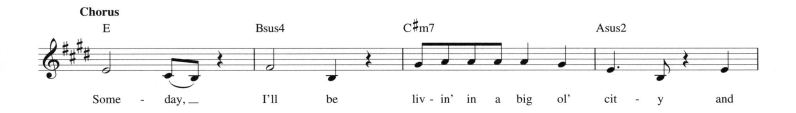

Some - day, ___ I'll be liv - in' in a big ol' cit - y and

all you're ___ ev - er gon - na be is mean.

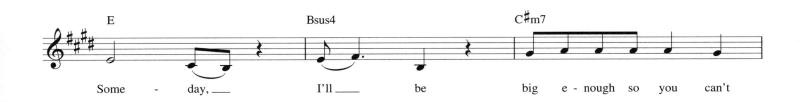

Some - day, ___ I'll ___ be big e - nough so you can't

hit me and all you're _____ ev - er gon - na be is

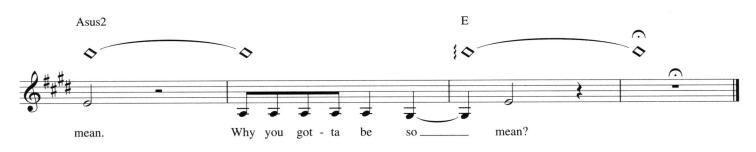

mean. Why you got - ta be so _____ mean?

Mine

Words and Music by Taylor Swift

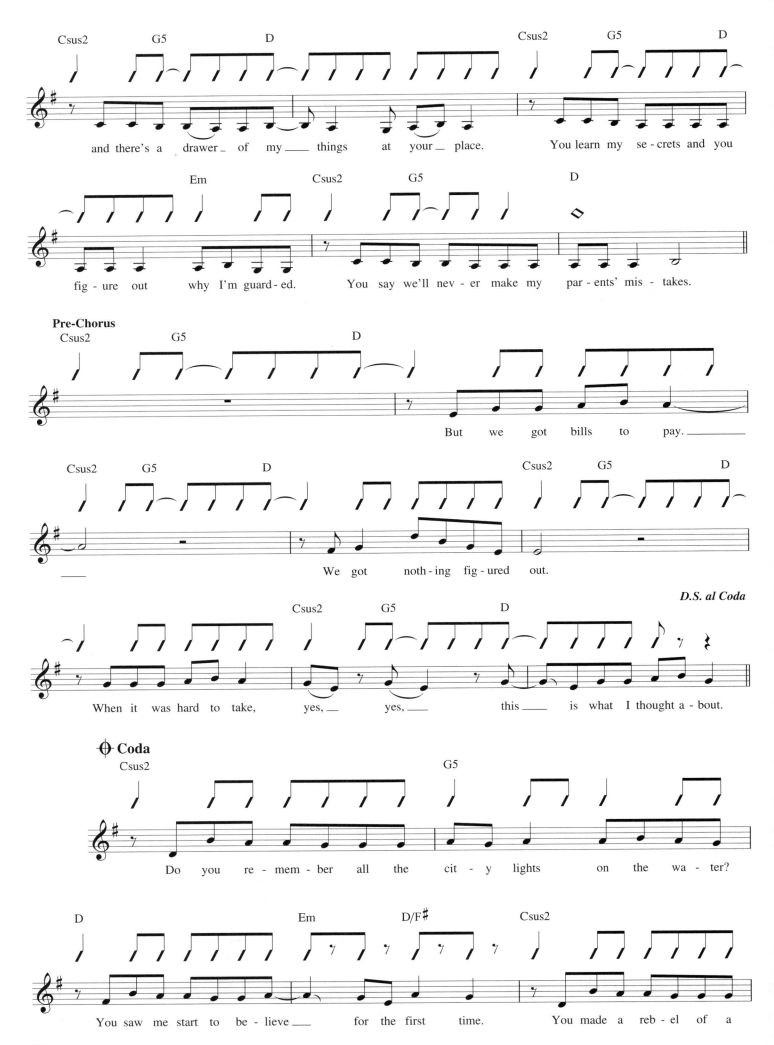

and there's a drawer of my ___ things at your ___ place. You learn my se - crets and you

fig - ure out why I'm guard - ed. You say we'll nev - er make my par - ents' mis - takes.

Pre-Chorus

But we got bills to pay. ___

We got noth - ing fig - ured out.

D.S. al Coda

When it was hard to take, yes, ___ yes, ___ this ___ is what I thought a - bout.

Coda

Do you re - mem - ber all the cit - y lights on the wa - ter?

You saw me start to be - lieve ___ for the first time. You made a reb - el of a

care-less man's care-ful daugh-ter. You are the best thing that's ev-er been mine. ___

Interlude

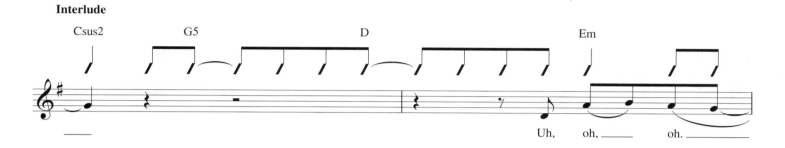

___ Uh, oh, ___ oh. ___

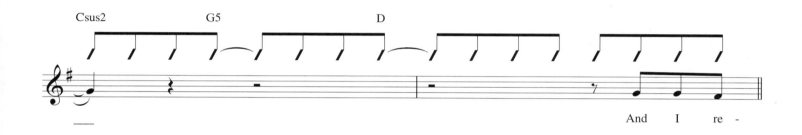

___ And I re -

Bridge

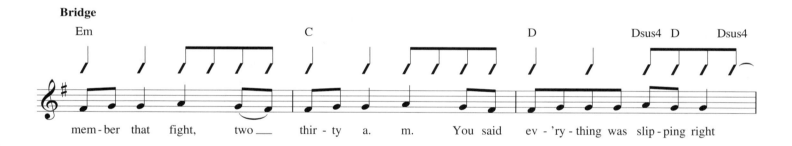

mem-ber that fight, two ___ thir-ty a. m. You said ev-'ry-thing was slip-ping right

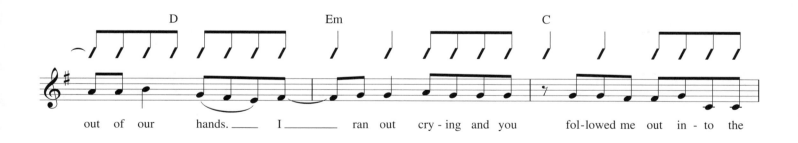

out of our hands. ___ I ___ ran out cry-ing and you fol-lowed me out in-to the

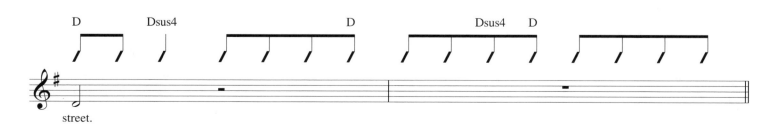

street.

Braced__ my - self for the good - bye _____ 'cause that's all__

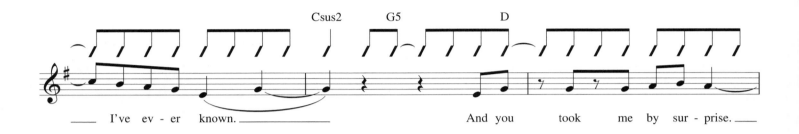

____ I've ev - er known. _____ And you took me by sur - prise. ____

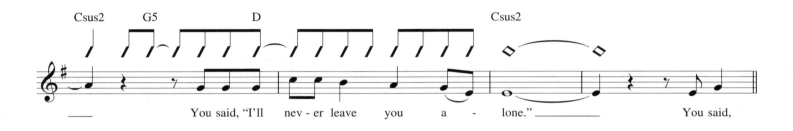

____ You said, "I'll nev - er leave you a - lone." _____ You said,

Outro-Chorus

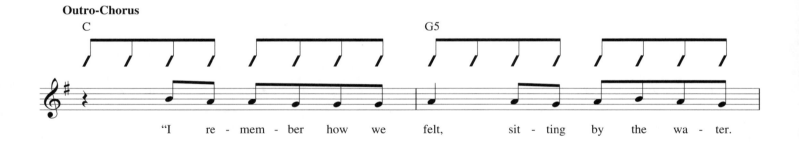

"I re - mem - ber how we felt, sit - ting by the wa - ter.

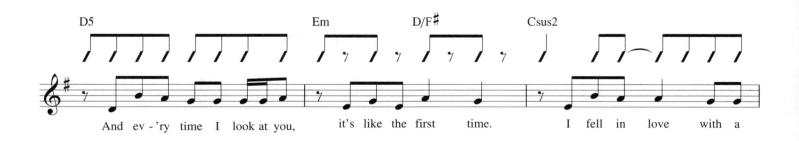

And ev - 'ry time I look at you, it's like the first time. I fell in love with a

care - less man's care - ful daugh - ter. She is the best thing that's ev - er been__ mine." __

Our Song

Words and Music by Taylor Swift

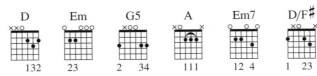

Intro
Moderately slow

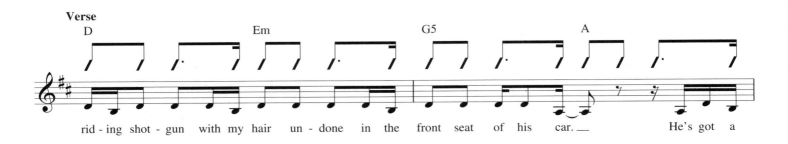

1. I was

Verse

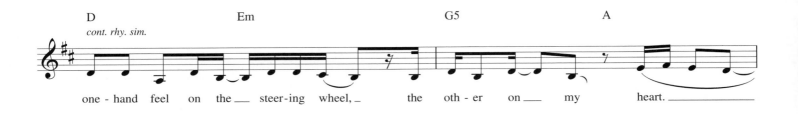

rid-ing shot-gun with my hair un-done in the front seat of his car. ___ He's got a

one-hand feel on the ___ steer-ing wheel, ___ the oth-er on ___ my heart. _____

___ I look a-round, turn the ra-di-o down. He says, "Ba-by, is some-thing wrong?" ___ I

say, "Noth-ing. I was just think-ing how we don't have ___ a song." ___ And he ___ says,

D   Em   G5   A

cont. rhy. sim.

gone all wrong __ and been tram - pled on __ and, uh, lost and thrown a - way. __

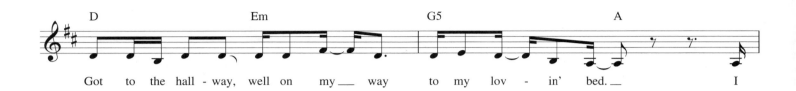

D   Em   G5   A

Got to the hall - way, well on my __ way to my lov - in' bed. __   I

D.S. al Coda

D   Em   G5   A

al - most did - n't no - tice all the ros - es and the note __ that said... __

⊕ Coda

Fiddle/Guitar Solo

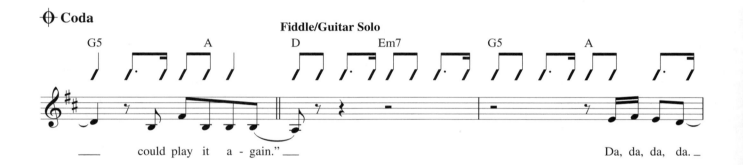

G5   A   D   Em7   G5   A

__ could play it a - gain." __   Da, da, da, da. __

D   Em7   G5

__

Bridge

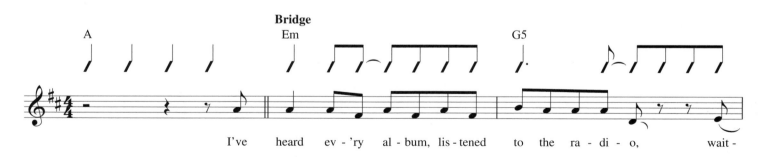

A   Em   G5

I've heard ev - 'ry al - bum, lis - tened to the ra - di - o,   wait -

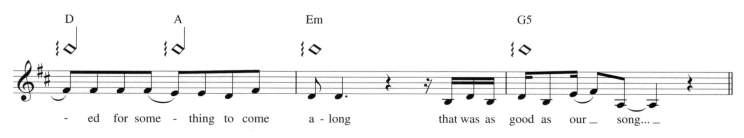

D   A   Em   G5

- ed for some - thing to come a - long that was as good as our __ song... __

Chorus

'Cause our song is the slam-ming screen door, sneak-in' out late, tap-ping on his, uh, win-

dow, when we're on the phone _ and he talks real slow 'cause it's late and his ma-ma don't

know. Our song is the way he laughs, _ the first date, "Man, I did-n't kiss him, and I should have."

And when I ___ got home, 'fore I said _ a - men, ask-ing God _ if he _

Interlude

___ could play it a - gain, _____ yeah. _____ Uh, play it a-

cont. rhy. sim.

gain, _____ oh, __ yeah. _____ Huh, __ oh, __

Outro

___ yeah. I was rid-ing shot-gun with my hair un-done in the front seat of his car. _

rit.

I grabbed a pen and an old nap-kin and I... wrote down our __ song.

Picture to Burn

Words and Music by Taylor Swift and Liz Rose

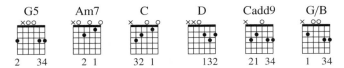

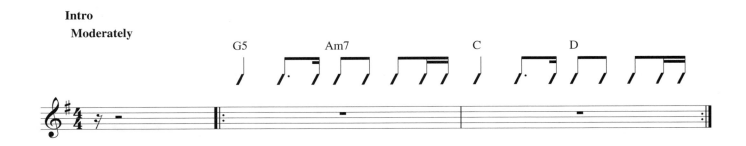

Intro
Moderately

Verse

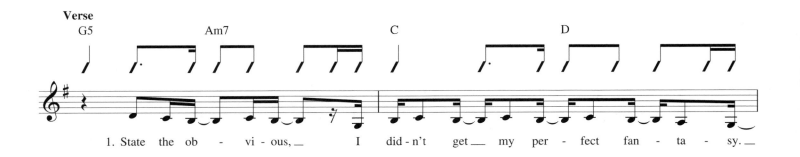

1. State the ob - vi - ous, ___ I did-n't get ___ my per - fect fan - ta - sy. ___

___ I re - al - ize ___ you love ___ your - self ___ more than you could ev - er love me. ___

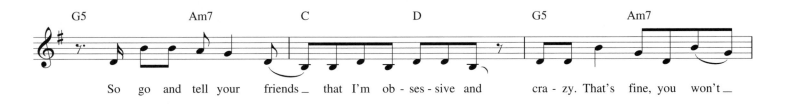

So go and tell your friends ___ that I'm ob - ses - sive and cra - zy. That's fine, you won't ___

mind if I say. ___ And by the way, ___ I hate ___ that

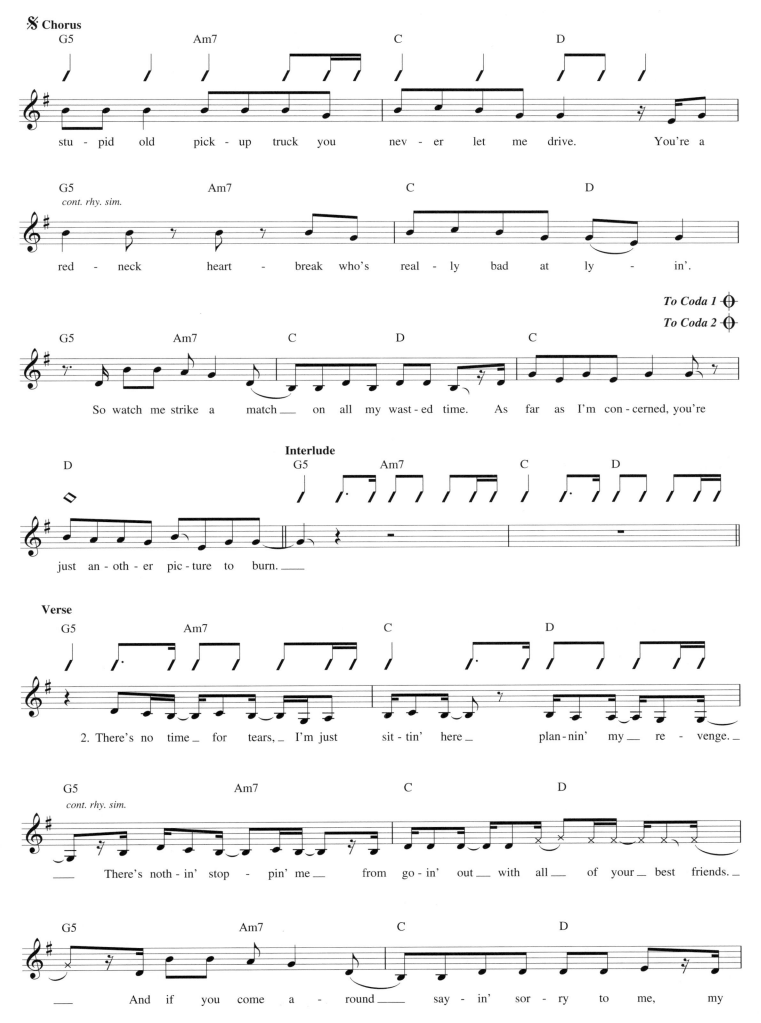

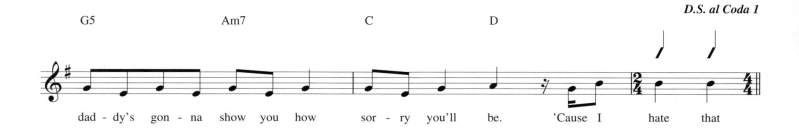

dad - dy's gon - na show you how sor - ry you'll be. 'Cause I hate that

Coda 1

Guitar Solo

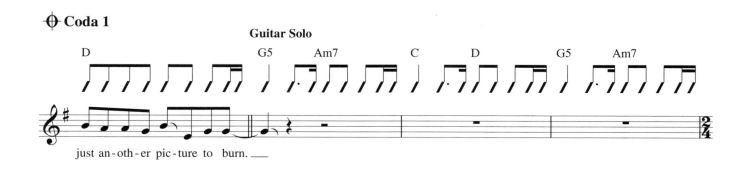

just an - oth - er pic - ture to burn. ___

Bridge

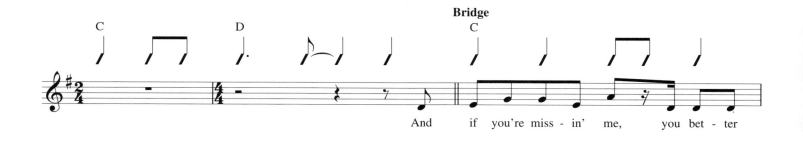

And if you're miss - in' me, you bet - ter

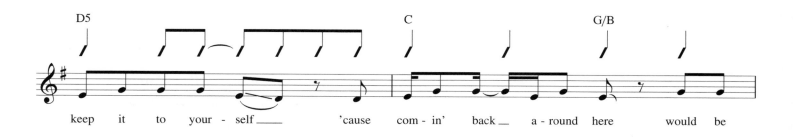

keep it to your - self ___ 'cause com - in' back ___ a - round here would be

bad for your health. _____ 'Cause I hate ___ that

Chorus

stu - pid old pick - up truck you nev - er let me drive. You're a

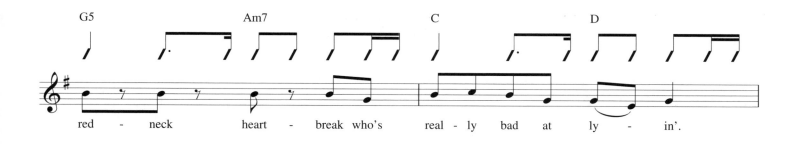

red - neck heart - break who's real - ly bad at ly - in'.

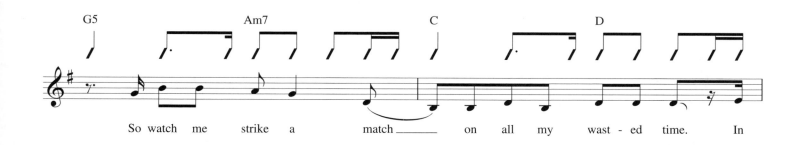

So watch me strike a match _____ on all my wast - ed time. In

D.S. al Coda 2

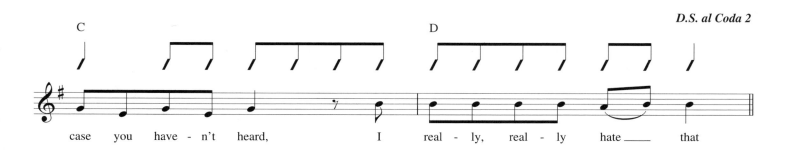

case you have - n't heard, I real - ly, real - ly hate _____ that

Coda 2

Outro

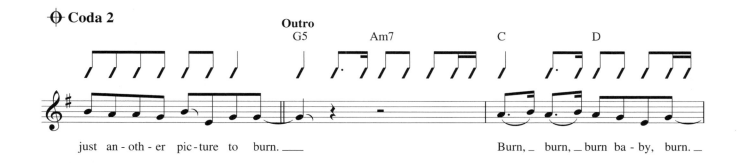

just an - oth - er pic - ture to burn. _____ Burn,__ burn,__ burn ba - by, burn.__

_____ You're just an - oth - er pic - ture to burn.__

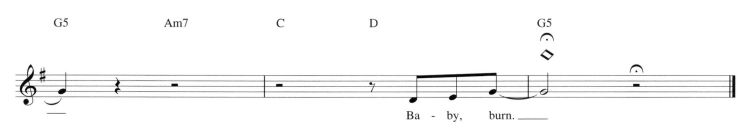

Ba - by, burn. _____

Red

Words and Music by Taylor Swift

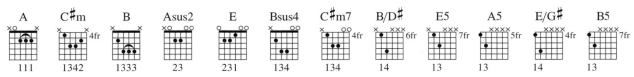

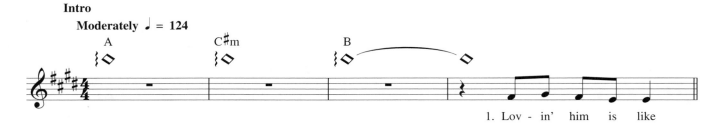

Intro

Moderately ♩ = 124

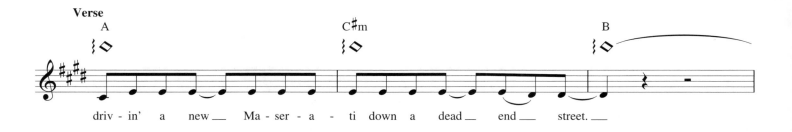

1. Lov - in' him is like

Verse

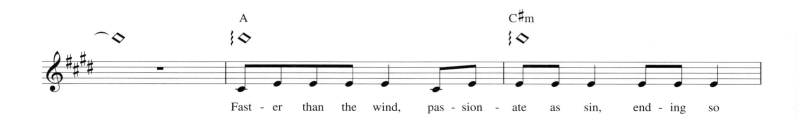

driv - in' a new __ Ma - ser - a - ti down a dead __ end __ street. __

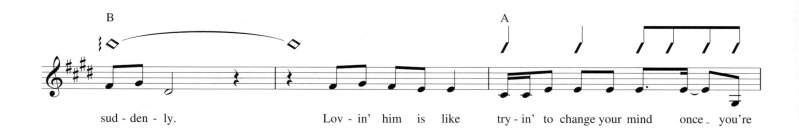

Fast - er than the wind, pas - sion - ate as sin, end - ing so

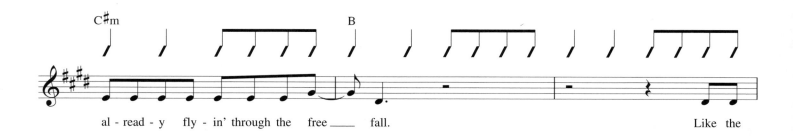

sud - den - ly. Lov - in' him is like try - in' to change your mind once __ you're

al - read - y fly - in' through the free __ fall. Like the

col - ors in au - tumn so bright ___ just be - fore they lose _____ it ___ all. _____

Chorus

___ Los - ing him was blue _ like I'd nev - er ___ known. _____ Miss - ing him was

dark grey, all a - lone. _____ For - get - ting him was like try - in' to know some - bod -

- y you nev - er ___ met. ___ But lov - in' him was

red. ___

Lov - in' him was red. ___

Verse

2. Touch - in' him was like re - al - iz - ing all you ev - er

Chorus

Sparks Fly

Words and Music by Taylor Swift

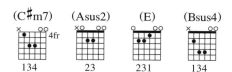

Capo I

Intro
Moderately fast

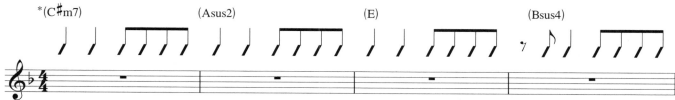

*Symbols in parentheses represent chord names respective to capoed guitar
and do not reflect actual sounding chords.

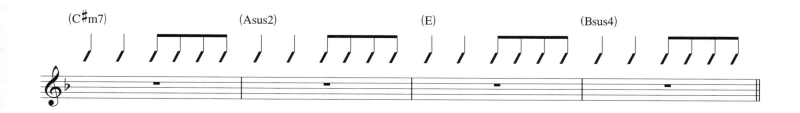

Verse

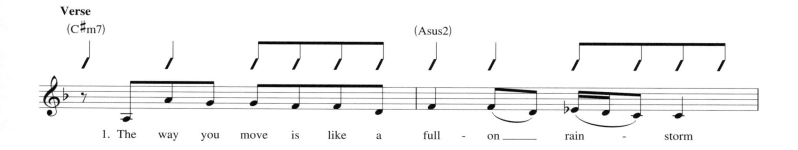

1. The way you move is like a full - on rain - storm

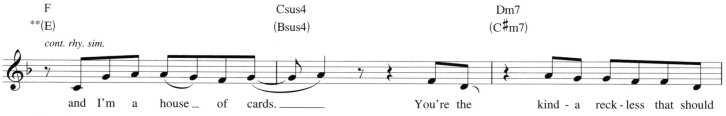

and I'm a house of cards. You're the kind - a reck - less that should

**Symbols in parentheses represent chord names respective to capoed guitar.
Symbols above reflect actual sounding chords.

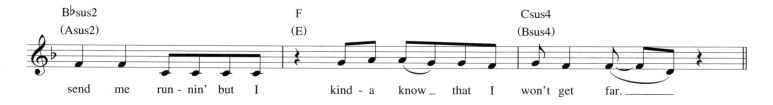

send me run - nin' but I kind - a know that I won't get far.

Pre-Chorus

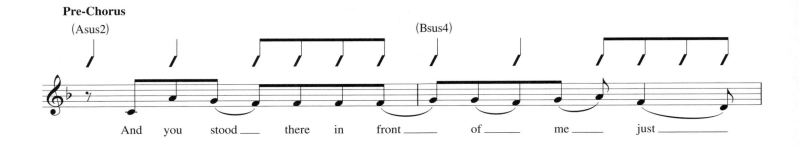

And you stood ___ there in front ___ of ___ me ___ just ___

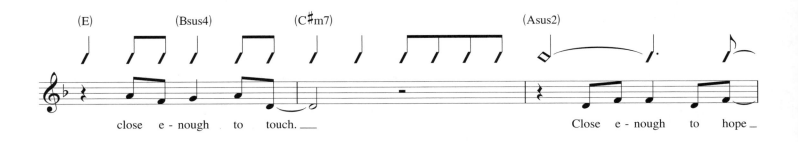

close e - nough to touch. ___ Close e - nough to hope ___

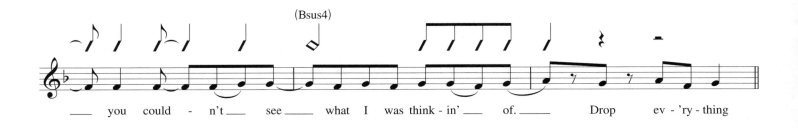

___ you could - n't ___ see ___ what I was think - in' ___ of. ___ Drop ev - 'ry - thing

𝄋 Chorus

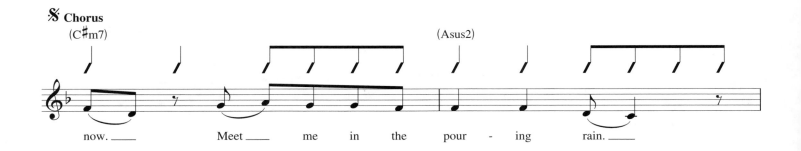

now. ___ Meet ___ me in the pour - ing rain. ___

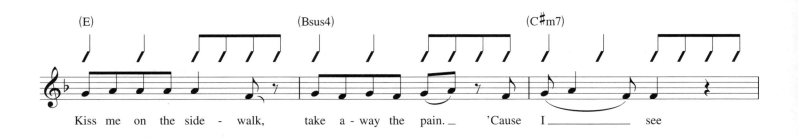

Kiss me on the side - walk, take a - way the pain. ___ 'Cause I ___ see

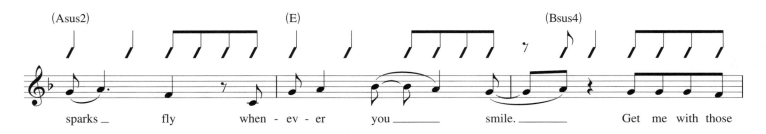

sparks ___ fly when - ev - er you ___ smile. ___ Get me with those

Pre-Chorus

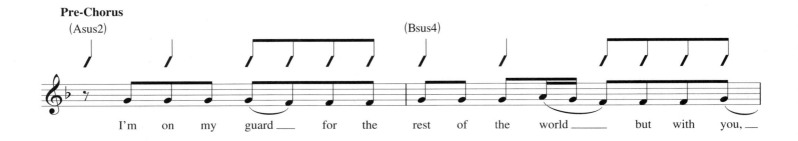

I'm on my guard ___ for the rest of the world ___ but with you, ___

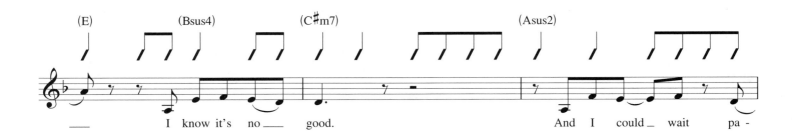

___ I know it's no ___ good. And I could ___ wait pa-

D.S. al Coda 1

- tient - ly ___ but ___ I real - ly wish you ___ would ___ drop ev - 'ry - thing

Coda 1

Interlude

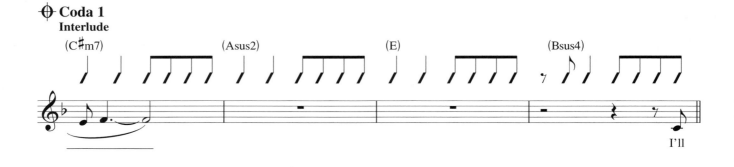

I'll

Bridge

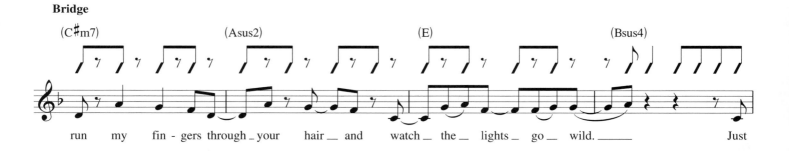

run my fin - gers through ___ your hair ___ and watch ___ the ___ lights ___ go ___ wild. ___ Just

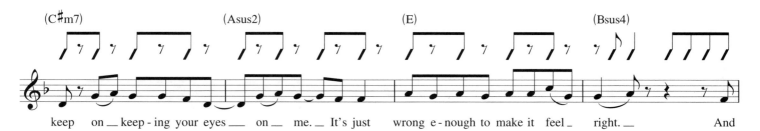

keep on ___ keep - ing your eyes ___ on ___ me. It's just wrong e - nough to make it feel ___ right. ___ And

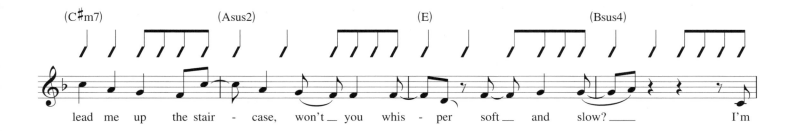

lead me up the stair - case, won't __ you whis - per soft __ and slow? ___ I'm

cap - ti - vat - ed by ___ you ba - by, like a fire - works __ show. Drop ev -'ry - thing

Chorus

now. Meet __ me in the pour - ing rain. Kiss me on the side - walk, take a - way the pain. __'Cause

D.S.S. al Coda 2

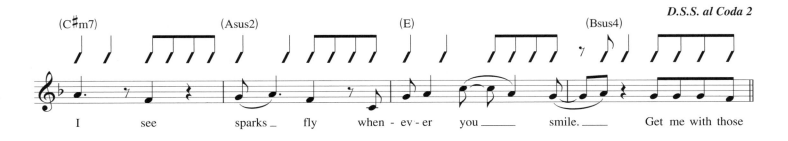

I see sparks __ fly when - ev - er you _____ smile. ___ Get me with those

Coda 2
Outro

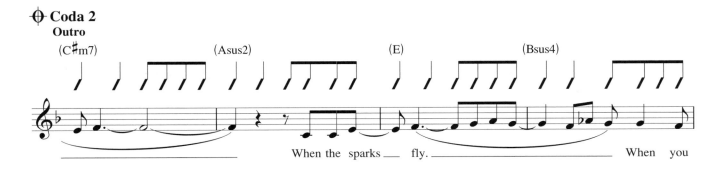

_____ When the sparks __ fly. _____ When you

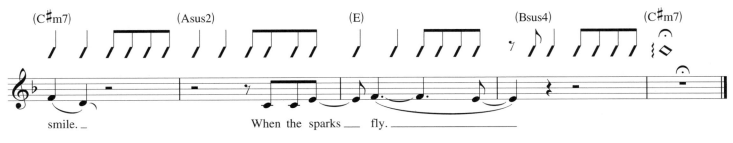

smile. _ When the sparks __ fly. _____

Should've Said No

Words and Music by Taylor Swift

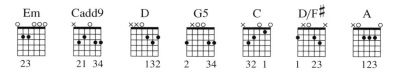

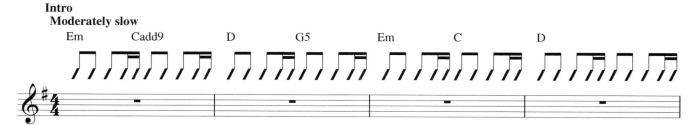

Intro
Moderately slow

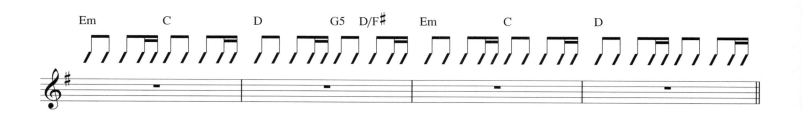

Verse

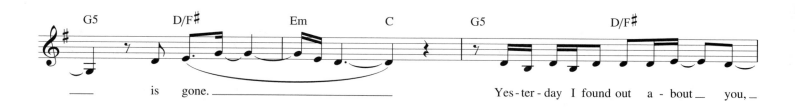

1. It's strange to think the songs _ we used _ to sing, _ the smiles, _ the flow - ers, ev - 'ry - thing... _

_ is gone. _____ Yes - ter - day I found out a - bout _ you, _

_ e - ven now just look - ing at _ you... feels wrong. _____

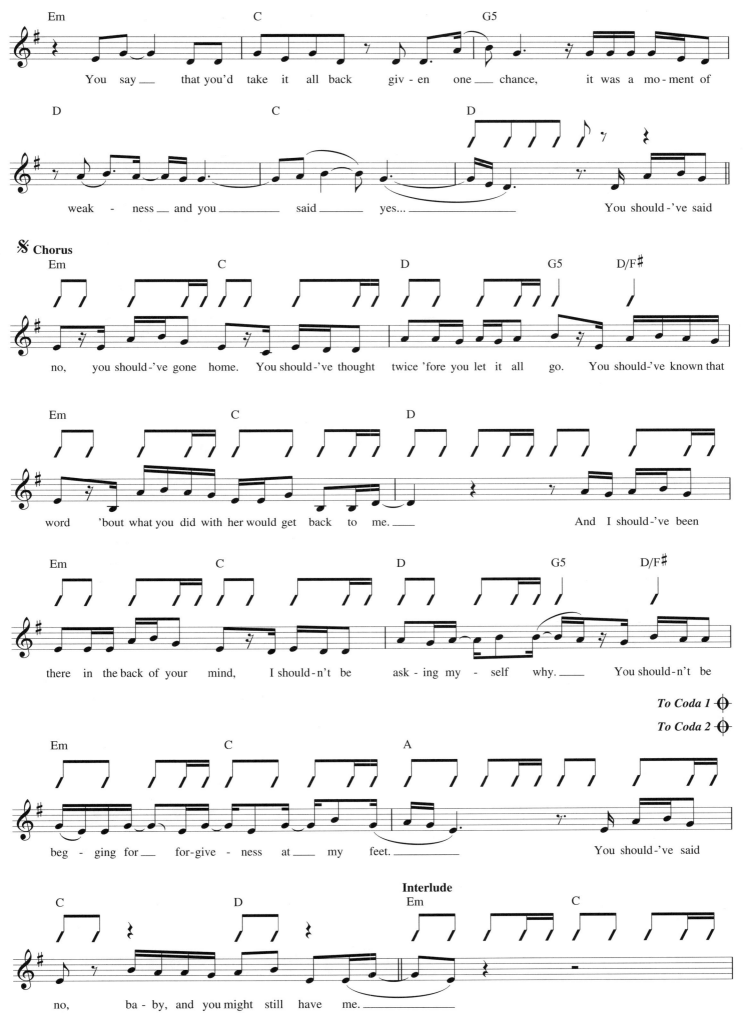

Verse

2. You can see that I've been cry - ing and, ba - by, you know all the right things...

to say. But do you hon - est - ly ex -

pect me to be - lieve we could ev - er be the same?

You say that the past is the past. You need one chance, it was a mo - ment of

D.S. al Coda 1

weak - ness and you said yes. You should -'ve said

Coda 1

Guitar Solo

no, ba - by, and you might still have me.

Oh, whoa.

The Story of Us

Words and Music by Taylor Swift

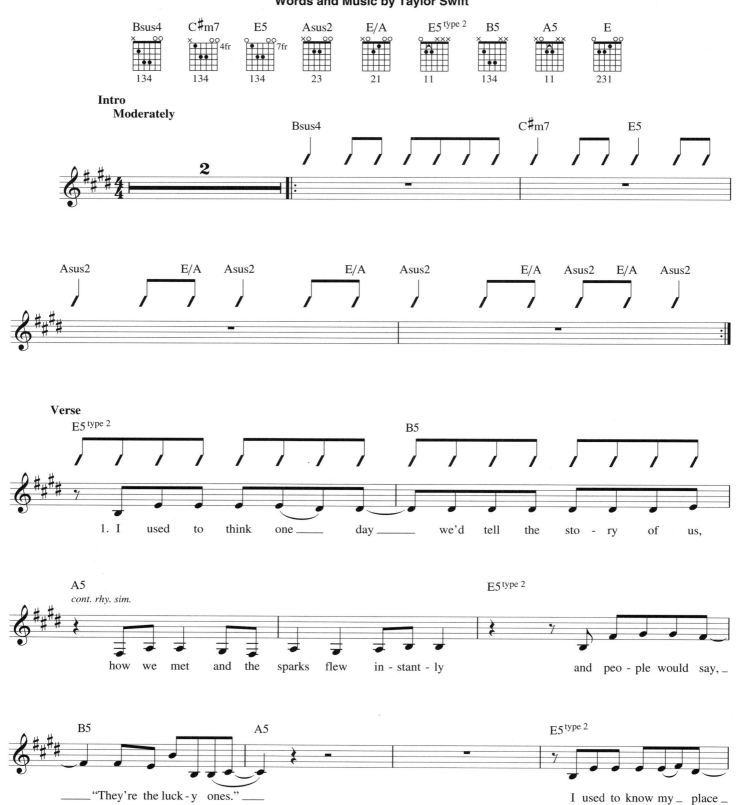

'cause late - ly I don't e - ven know what page you're on.

Pre-Chorus

Oh, a sim - ple com - pli - ca - tion, mis - com - mu - ni -

ca - tions lead to fall - out. So man - y things that I

wish you knew. So man - y walls up, I can't break through.

Chorus

Now I'm stand - ing a - lone in a crowd - ed room.

and we're not speak - in'.

And I'm dy - in' to know, is it kill - in' you

like it's kill - in' me? Yeah. I don't know what to say

since the twist of fate when it all broke down. And the

To Coda 2 ⊕   *To Coda 1* ⊕

sto - ry of us looks a lot like a trag - e - dy now. Next chap - ter.

Interlude

Verse

2. How'd we end up this way? See me nerv - ous - ly pull -

- ing at my clothes and try - in' to look bus - y

and you're do - in' your best to a - void me.

I'm start - ing to think one day I'll tell the sto - ry of us,

Outro-Chorus

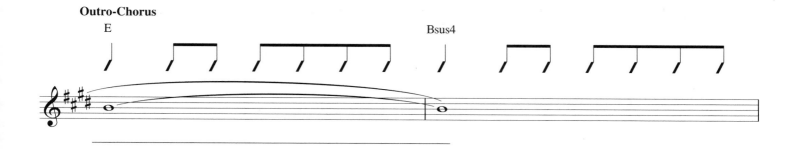

E   Bsus4

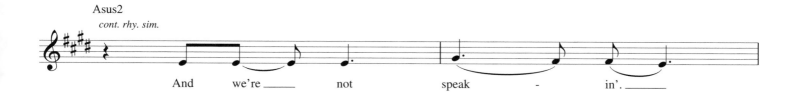

Asus2
cont. rhy. sim.

And we're _____ not speak - in'. _____

E   Bsus4   Asus2

And I'm dy - in' to know, _____ is it kill - in' you like it's kill - in' _____

C#m7   Bsus4

me? _____ Yeah. _____ I don't know what to say _____ since the twist of

E   Asus2   C#m7

fate, 'cause we're go - in' down. And the sto - ry of us _____ looks a

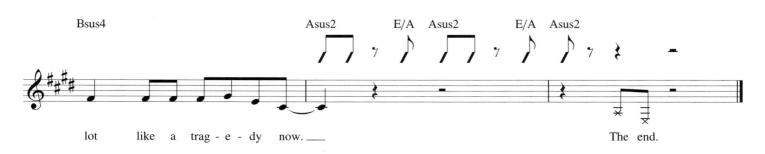

Bsus4   Asus2   E/A Asus2   E/A Asus2

lot like a trag - e - dy now. _____   The end.

Teardrops on My Guitar

Words and Music by Taylor Swift and Liz Rose

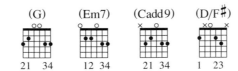

Capo III

Intro
Moderately slow

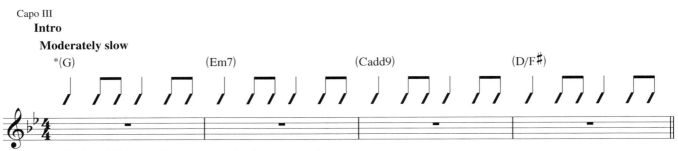

*Chord symbols in parentheses represent chord names respective
to capoed guitar and do not reflect actual sounding chords.

Verse

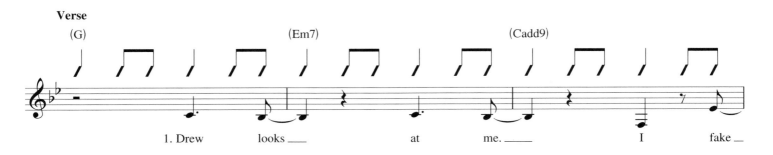

1. Drew looks ___ at me. ___ I fake ___

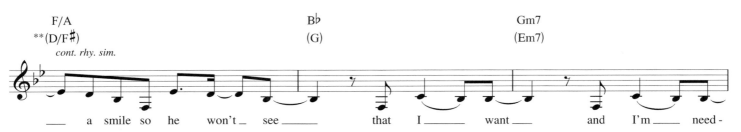

___ a smile so he won't ___ see ___ that I ___ want ___ and I'm ___ need-

**Symbols in parentheses represent chord names respective to capoed guitar.
Symbols above reflect actual sounding chords.

- ing ___ ev - 'ry - thing that we should ___ be. ___ I'll bet she's beau - ti - ful,

that girl he talks a - bout. And she's got ev - 'ry - thing that I had to live with - out.

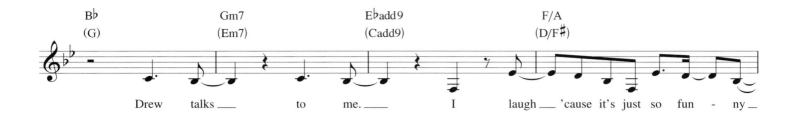

Drew talks ___ to me. ___ I laugh ___ 'cause it's just so fun - ny ___

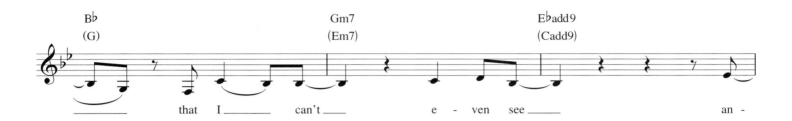

___ that I ___ can't ___ e - ven see ___ an -

- y - one when he's with ___ me. ___ He says he's so in love, he's fi - n'lly got it right.

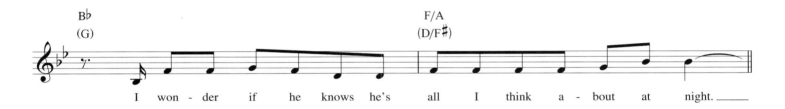

I won - der if he knows he's all I think a - bout at night. ___

%̶ Chorus

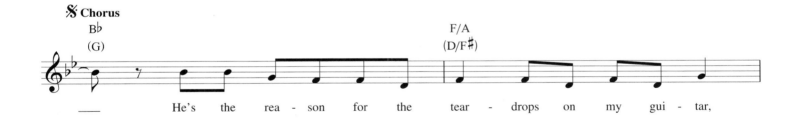

___ He's the rea - son for the tear - drops on my gui - tar,

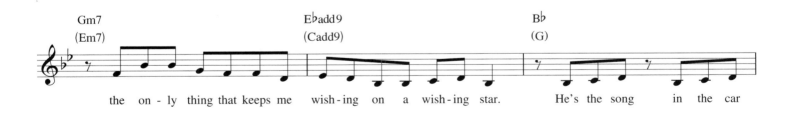

the on - ly thing that keeps me wish-ing on a wish-ing star. He's the song in the car

To Coda ⊕

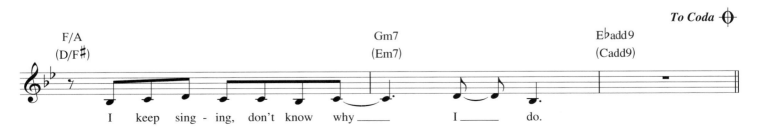

I keep sing - ing, don't know why ___ I ___ do.

Verse

Bb (G) / Gm7 (Em7) / Ebadd9 (Cadd9)

2. Drew walks ____ by ____ me. ____ Can —

F/A (D/F#) / Bb (G) / Gm7 (Em7)

— he tell that I ___ can't _ breathe? ____ And there he ___ goes ___ so per - fect - ly, —

Ebadd9 (Cadd9) / F/A (D/F#) / Gm7 (Em7)

____ the kind of flaw - less I wish I could be. She bet - ter hold him tight,

D.S. al Coda

Ebadd9 (Cadd9) / Bb (G) / F/A (D/F#)

give him all her love, look in those beau - ti - ful ___ eyes ____ and know she's luck - y 'cause ___

Coda

Guitar Solo

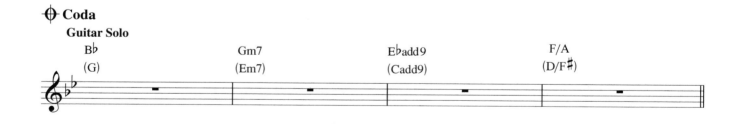

Bb (G) / Gm7 (Em7) / Ebadd9 (Cadd9) / F/A (D/F#)

Pre-Chorus

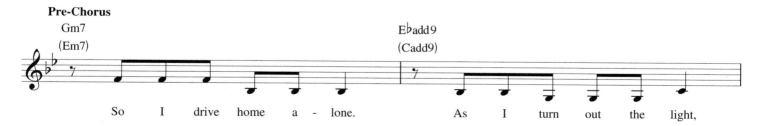

Gm7 (Em7) / Ebadd9 (Cadd9)

So I drive home a - lone. As I turn out the light,

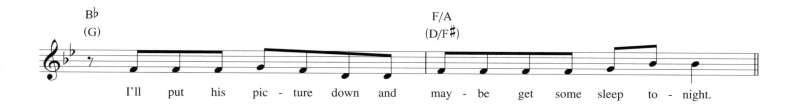

Bb
(G)

F/A
(D/F#)

I'll put his pic - ture down and may - be get some sleep to - night.

Chorus

Bb
(G)

F/A
(D/F#)

Gm7
(Em7)

'Cause he's the rea - son for the tear - drops on my gui - tar, the on - ly one who's got e -

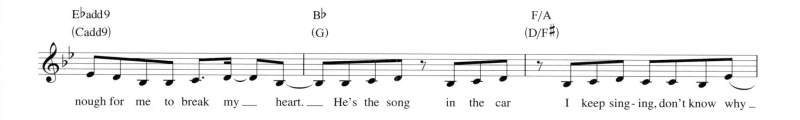

Ebadd9
(Cadd9)

Bb
(G)

F/A
(D/F#)

nough for me to break my ___ heart. ___ He's the song in the car I keep sing - ing, don't know why ___

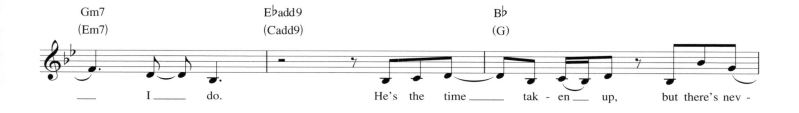

Gm7
(Em7)

Ebadd9
(Cadd9)

Bb
(G)

___ I ___ do. He's the time ___ tak - en ___ up, but there's nev -

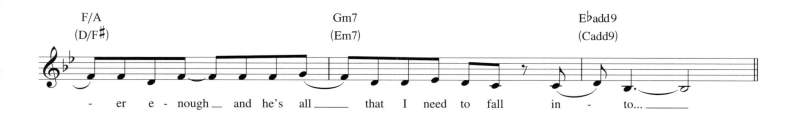

F/A
(D/F#)

Gm7
(Em7)

Ebadd9
(Cadd9)

- er e - nough ___ and he's all ___ that I need to fall in - to... ___

Outro

(G)　　　　(Em7)　　　　(Cadd9)　　　　(D/F#)　　　　(G)

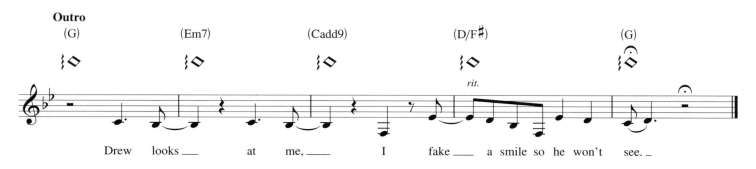

rit.

Drew looks ___ at me, ___ I fake ___ a smile so he won't see. ___

We Are Never Ever Getting Back Together

Words and Music by Taylor Swift, Shellback and Max Martin

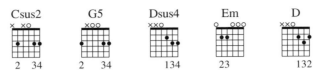

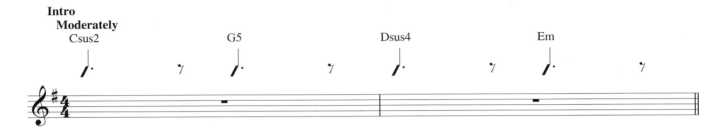

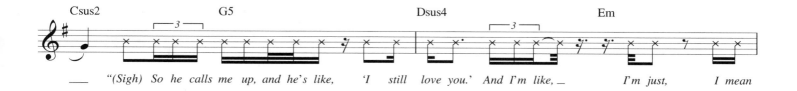

Csus2   G5   Dsus4   Em

___ "(Sigh) So he calls me up, and he's like, 'I still love you.' And I'm like, ___ I'm just, I mean

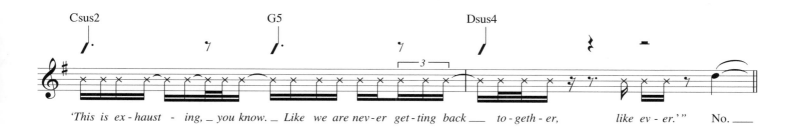

Csus2   G5   Dsus4

'This is ex-haust-ing, ___ you know. ___ Like we are nev-er get-ting back ___ to-geth-er, like ev-er.'" No. ___

Outro-Chorus

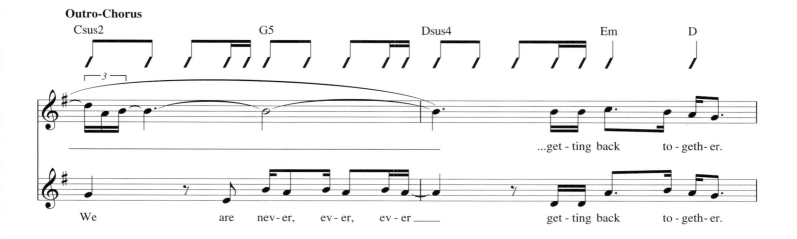

Csus2   G5   Dsus4   Em   D

...get-ting back to-geth-er.

We   are nev-er, ev-er, ev-er ___ get-ting back to-geth-er.

Csus2   G5   Dsus4   Em   D

cont. rhy. sim.

Uh, ___ oo. ___

We... ___ ...are nev-er, ev-er, ev-er ___ get-ting back to-geth-er.

Csus2   G5   Dsus4   Em   D

You go talk to your ___ friends, talk to my ___ friends, ...to me. ___

You go talk to your ___ friends, talk to my ___ friends, talk to me. ___ But

...nev – er, ev – er, ev – er ev – er getting back to-

we... ___

...are nev – er, ev – er, ev – er, ___ ev – er getting back to-

geth-er. ___ No.

Oo, ___ oo, oo. ___ Oo, ___ oo, oo. ___ (Oo.)

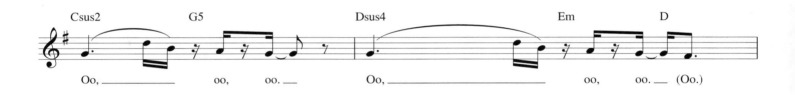

Oo, ___ oo, oo. ___ Oo, ___ oo, oo. ___ (Oo.)

You go talk to your ___ friends, talk to my ___ friends, talk to me. ___ But

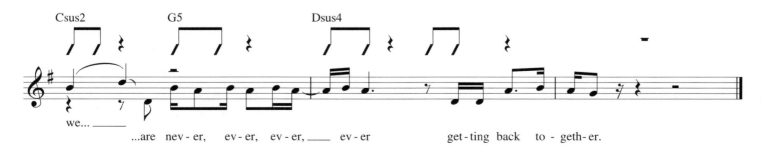

we... ___

...are nev – er, ev – er, ev – er, ___ ev – er get-ting back to-geth-er.

78

White Horse

Words and Music by Taylor Swift and Liz Rose

Intro
Moderately slow

1. Say you're sor - ry, that face ___ of an an - gel comes out ___ just when you need it to,

cont. rhy. sim.

as I paced ___ back and forth ___ all this time ___ 'cause I

hon - est - ly be - lieved in ___ you. Hold - ing on, the days ___ drag on. Stu - pid girl,

I should-'ve known, I should-'ve known ___ that I'm not a prin -

Chorus

- cess, this ain't a fair - y tale. I'm not the one ___

My mis - take, ___ I did - n't know to be in love ___ you had to fight to have the up - per hand. I had so man - y dreams a - bout you ___ and me. ___ Hap - py end - ings, now ___ I know ___ that I'm not a prin -

D.S. al Coda

Coda

___ late for you ___ and your white ___ horse to come a - round. ___

Interlude

Bridge

And there you are on your ___ knees,

beg - ging for for - give - ness, beg - ging for me.

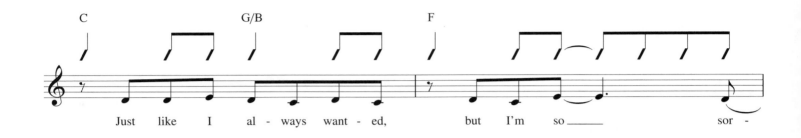

Just like I al - ways want - ed, but I'm so ___ sor -

- ry... ____ 'Cause I'm not your prin -

Chorus

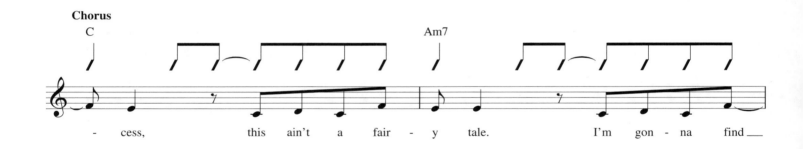

- cess, this ain't a fair - y tale. I'm gon - na find ___

cont. rhy. sim.

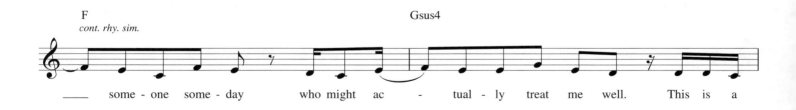

___ some - one some - day who might ac - tual - ly treat me well. This is a

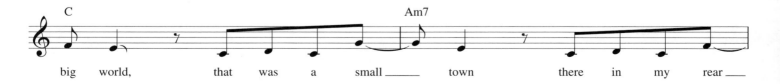

big world, that was a small ___ town there in my rear ___

_____ view mir - ror dis - ap - pear - ing now. _____ And it's too _____

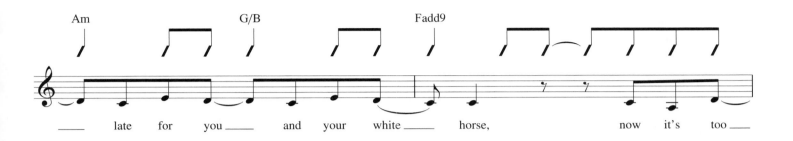

_____ late for you _____ and your white _____ horse, now it's too _____

_____ late for you _____ and your white _____ horse to catch me _____

Outro

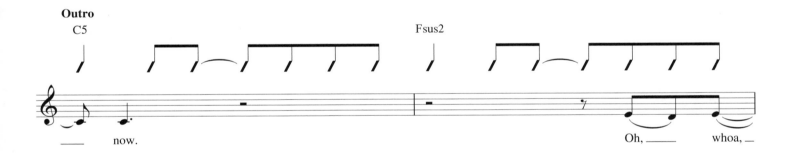

_____ now. Oh, _____ whoa, _____

_____ whoa, _ whoa. _____ Try and catch _ me _ now, _____ oh. _____

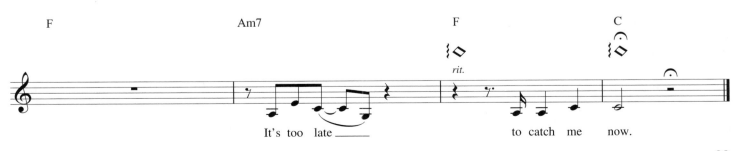

It's too late _____ to catch me now.

You Belong with Me

Words and Music by Taylor Swift and Liz Rose

Tune down 1/2 step:
(low to high) Eb-Ab-Db-Gb-Bb-Eb

Intro
Moderately

Verse

1. You're on the phone with your girl-friend, she's up-set. ___ She's go-ing off a-bout some-thing that ___ you said ___ 'cause she does-n't get your hu-mor like I do.

I'm in the room, it's a typ-i-cal Tues-day night. ___ I'm lis-t'ning to the kind of mu-sic she does-n't like, ___ and she'll nev-er know your sto-ry like I do. But

Verse

G5

2. Walk in the streets with you _____ and your worn out _____ jeans, _____

D   Am

cont. rhy. sim.

_____ I can't help think-ing this is how it ought _ to _ be. _ Laugh-ing on a park

C

bench, think-ing to my-self, _ "Hey, is-n't this eas - y?" _ And you've got a smile that could

D

light up this whole _ town. _____ I have-n't seen it in a while since she brought you down. _

Am   C

_____ You say you're fine, I know you bet-ter than that. Hey, what you do-ing with a

Pre-Chorus

Am   C   G5

girl like that? She wears high heels, I wear sneak-ers. She's cheer cap-tain and

D   Am   C

I'm on the bleach-ers, dream-ing 'bout the day when you wake up and find_ that what you're

D

look-ing for has been here _____ the whole time. If you could

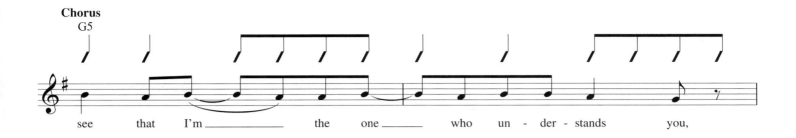

see that I'm _____ the one _____ who un - der - stands you,

been here all _____ a - long. _____ So why can't you see, _____ ee, _____

_____ you be - long _____ with me, _____ ee? _____

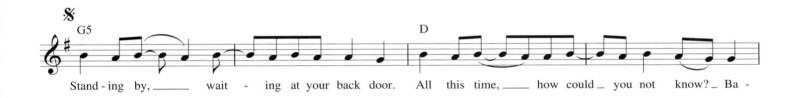

Stand - ing by, _____ wait - ing at your back door. All this time, _____ how could _____ you not know? _____ Ba -

To Coda ⊕

by, _____ ee, _____ you be - long _____ with me, _____ ee. _____ You be - long _____ with me. _____

Guitar Solo

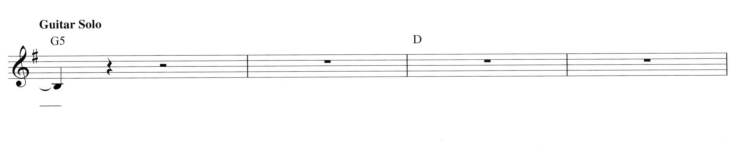

Oh, _____ I re - mem - ber you